RULERS AND THEIR TIMES

# CHARLEMAGNE
## and the Early Middle Ages

by Miriam Greenblatt

**BENCHMARK BOOKS**

MARSHALL CAVENDISH
NEW YORK

ACKNOWLEDGMENT

With thanks to Professor John J. Contreni, Department of History, Purdue University, for his thoughtful reading of the manuscript

Benchmark Books
Marshall Cavendish
99 White Plains Road
Tarrytown, New York 10591-9001
www.marshallcavendish.com
Text copyright © 2003 by Miriam Greenblatt

Map © 2003 by Marshall Cavendish Corporation
Map by Rodica Prato

Library of Congress Cataloging-in-Publication Data
Greenblatt, Miriam.
Charlemagne and the early Middle Ages / by Miriam Greenblatt.
p. cm. — (Rulers and their times)
Summary: Provides an overview of the lives of Charlemagne and his subjects in the Frankish empire of the late eighth and early ninth centuries, and includes excerpts from poems, letters, laws, and biographies of the time.
Includes bibliographical references and index.
ISBN 0-7614-1487-8
1. Charlemagne, Emperor, 742–814—Juvenile literature. 2. France—Kings and rulers—Biography—Juvenile literature. 3. Holy Roman Empire—Kings and rulers—Biography—Juvenile literature. 4. France—History—To 987—Juvenile literature. 5. Holy Roman Empire—History—To 1517—Juvenile literature. 6. Civilization, Medieval—Juvenile literature. [1. Charlemagne, Emperor, 742–814. 2. Kings, queens, rulers, etc. 3. France—History—To 987. 4. Holy Roman Empire—History—To 1517. 5. Civilization, Medieval.] I. Title. II. Series.
DC73 .G74    2003    944'.014—dc21    2002001973

Picture Research by Linda Sykes Picture Research, Hilton Head, SC
Cover: Louvre/Erich Lessing/Art Resource NY; page 5: Stadtmuseum, Aachen, France/Superstock; pages 6–7, Bibliotheque de L'Arsenal, Paris/Explorer, Paris/Superstock; pages 8, 9, 18, 26: Bibliotheque Nationale, Paris/AKG London; page 13: DY/Art Resource NY; page 15: Bibliotheque Nationale, Paris Ms. Fr. 2813 fol. 121; page 17: Prado, Madrid/Scala/Art Resource NY; page 20: Private Collection/Bridgeman Art Library International; page 23: Musee Conde, Chantilly, France/Bridgeman Art Library International; page 25: Bibliotheque Nationale, Paris/ Bridgeman Art Library International; Page 28: Austrian Nationalbibliothek, Vienna/AKG London; pages 31, 35: Musee Conde, Chantilly/Giraudon/Art Resource NY; pages 36–37: Bibliotheque de L'Arsenal, Paris/Giraudon/Bridgeman Art Library International; Page 39: Bayerische Staatsbibliothek, Munich/AKG London; pages 41, 61: Erich Lessing/Art Resource NY; page 44: Uffizi, Florence/Scala/Art Resource NY; page 46: Giraudon/Art Resource NY; pages 49, 60: The Art Archive; page 53: AKG London; page 56: Superstock; page 61: Erich Lessing/Art Resource NY; pages 66–67: Saechsische Landesbiblithek, Dresden, Germany/AKG London; page 69: British Library/ AKG London; pages 72, 75: Bridgeman Art Library International

Printed in Hong Kong
135642

# Contents

# Charles the Great, King of the Franks

Some fifteen hundred years ago, during the fourth and fifth centuries, the Roman Empire, which had controlled most of Europe and the Middle East, split in two. The eastern part became the Byzantine Empire and lasted for more than one thousand years. The western part turned into dozens of small kingdoms ruled by various Germanic tribes that had migrated there from northern and central Europe. By 800, most of the kingdoms were again united in a single empire, ruled by the Germanic Franks. Today most of this land consists of the nations of France, Germany, Switzerland, and Italy.

The man primarily responsible for creating the new empire was Charles the Great, commonly known by his French name of Charlemagne (Karl der Grosse to the Germans, Carolus Magnus to his Latin-speaking officials). He combined fighting skill with a real talent for governing. Deeply devoted to the Christian religion, he was also interested in education, literature, and art. The fame he gained during his lifetime continued after his death. He likely inspired more songs and legends than any other figure in European history.

In this book, you will learn about Charlemagne's battles and the changes he brought about in his kingdom, which have affected

Throughout his reign, Charlemagne encouraged the construction of churches and monasteries. Here he holds a model of the chapel built at his capital city of Aachen.

Europe to this very day. You will read about the life of a monk and that of a peasant, about the clothes the Franks wore, the foods they ate, and what they did for entertainment. Finally, you will read poems, letters, laws, and biographies in which the Franks themselves tell us about the early medieval world.

# PART ONE

Hundreds of years after he ruled, Charlemagne was still inspiring legends, poetry, and art. This fifteenth-century painting recalls his prowess in battle, but the famous leader was also admired for the strides he made in religion and learning.

# A Mighty Monarch

# Early Years

Born in 742, Charlemagne was the elder son of King Pepin III, also know as Pepin the Short, and Queen Bertrada of the kingdom of Frankland. As a boy, Charlemagne learned to swim, to ride horseback, and to hunt. He learned how to read and write, which was very unusual for that time. In addition to his native tongue of German, he learned Latin—both the formal Latin used in writing and the ordinary Latin that was evolving into French. He even picked up a few words of Greek.

Charlemagne also learned many other things that proved important in later years. He always accompanied his father's court as it traveled from one royal estate to another. In those years, a ruler such as King Pepin did not live in a capital city. It was easier to eat the food and use up the goods in one place and then move on than it was to transport supplies over bad roads. Also, it was useful for a ruler to be seen by as many of his subjects as possible. As a result of this moving around,

Charlemagne's father, Pepin III, was the first Frankish king to claim that he ruled by divine right.

Charlemagne became familiar with the kingdom he would one day rule. He attended the assemblies at which Frankish nobles discussed problems, voted on the king's decrees, and prepared for war. Thus he became comfortable about dealing with others.

When Charlemagne was just eleven years old, he rode out to welcome Pope Stephen II to Frankland. The pope had come to ask Pepin's help in fighting a Germanic tribe called the Lombards, who were threatening to capture Rome. During the visit, the pope anointed Pepin, Charlemagne, and his younger brother, Carloman, naming them the Three Kings of the Franks. He also forbade the Franks from choosing any king who did not belong to this family. Meeting the pope strengthened Charlemagne's determination to defend the Christian faith.

Charlemagne began his military career in his early teens. He joined his father on a campaign to Italy, where the Franks defeated the Lombards. The young prince also joined his father on several campaigns into Aquitaine, in what is now southwestern France. Here, too, the Franks were victorious.

The campaigns in Italy and Aquitaine did more than give Charlemagne experience in warfare. They exposed him to the remains of Roman civilization—its art, architecture, literature, music, and medicine. From then on, his interest in culture grew.

**Judging from her nickname of Big-foot Bertha, Charlemagne's mother, Bertrada, was apparently very tall.**

# The Young King

In 768, Pepin III died, and Frankland was divided between Charlemagne and Carloman. In separate but identical coronation ceremonies, each man was lifted up into the air on the shields of his nobles, as spears clashed and the people cried out, "May the king live forever."

The joint kingship, however, proved unworkable. The two brothers had never liked or trusted each other. When Charlemagne asked Carloman to help him put down an uprising in Aquitaine, Carloman refused. So Charlemagne marched on Aquitaine alone—and defeated the rebels in just two months. He then adopted a new method of ruling a conquered people. In the past, it had been customary to leave an army of occupation in a conquered area and wait for the next revolt to occur. Charlemagne decided instead to let the Aquitainians rule themselves according to their old laws and traditions. All he required was that they help the Franks in war. The method was a success and set the pattern for many of Charlemagne's future conquests.

The antagonism between the two brothers greatly disturbed their mother, who preferred Charlemagne to Carloman. Accordingly, Bertrada suggested to Charlemagne that he divorce his first wife, Himiltrude, and marry Gerperga, a daughter of the king of the Lombards. That would give Charlemagne an ally south of Carloman's territory. Charlemagne's own lands lay north and west of Carloman's territory. Thus the marriage would encircle and isolate the younger king.

As it turned out, the marriage to Gerperga lasted less than a year. What apparently happened was this. First, the pope sent Charlemagne a furious letter cursing the new marriage and asking the king how he dared ally himself with "the faithless and stinking Lombards, who cannot even be called a nation and who have brought leprosy into the world." Then Carloman fell ill and died. Charlemagne promptly marched his troops across the border and seized his brother's lands. With Frankland once again a unified kingdom, there was no reason for Charlemagne to stay married to Gerperga. Accordingly, he divorced her, sent her home to her father, and took a third wife, a Frankish girl named Hildegarde the Fair. Enraged at Charlemagne's treatment of his daughter, the Lombard king threatened war.

# A Series of Conquests

Although the pope urged Charlemagne to attack the Lombards at once, the king decided to first strike at the Saxons, a Germanic tribe that lived northeast of Frankland. Unlike the Franks, the Saxons had never converted to Christianity. They still worshipped pagan gods such as Thor and Woden. They sacrificed animals and cremated their dead. They still believed that spirits inhabited every river, rock, and tree. They also spent a great deal of time raiding Frankish settlements, burning their crops and destroying their churches.

To Charlemagne, defeating the Saxons meant striking a blow both for Christianity and for secure borders. So in 772, following the example of his father and grandfather, he launched a campaign against the Saxons. Moving rapidly, he soon reached their sacred grove, deep in the heart of a forest. There he cut down the Irminsul (an ancient, elaborately carved tree that held great symbolic importance to the Saxons) and seized the gold and silver offerings the Saxons had been depositing nearby for centuries. The Saxons then asked for peace, and Charlemagne withdrew, taking with him only a dozen hostages for the Saxons' good behavior.

The following year, the king turned his attention to the Lombards. After defeating them at a battlesite in northern Italy, he attacked their capital of Pavia. But the city was heavily fortified, and the Franks had no catapults, siege towers, or other assault weapons. Accordingly, Charlemagne and his troops set up a blockade and settled down to starve the Lombards out.

Autumn passed into winter, and winter into spring, and still Pavia did not surrender. Charlemagne, however, was so confident of ultimate victory that he decided to make an Easter pilgrimage to Rome. There he attended services and visited the tomb of Saint Peter. He also made friends with the new pope, Hadrian I, and vowed to do all he could to restore the city's ancient glory.

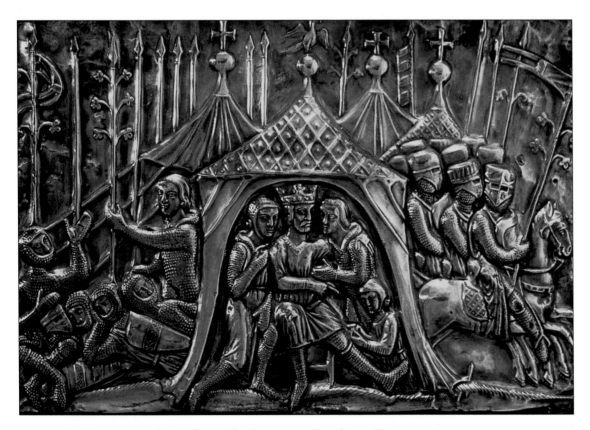

In his tent on a battlefield, Charlemagne plans his military strategy.

Charlemagne then returned to the siege of Pavia, which finally surrendered in the summer of 774. The Lombard king was packed off to spend the rest of his life in a monastery, after which Charlemagne had himself crowned King of the Lombards. He then granted Lombardy the same peace terms he had given Aquitaine. The people could rule themselves according to their old laws and traditions as long as they helped the Franks in war.

Next, Charlemagne resumed his struggle with the Saxons. He would invade Saxony, win some victories, convert some Saxons to Christianity, and leave. The Saxons would revert to their pagan beliefs and resume their raids on Frankish forts and churches. Charlemagne would again invade Saxony, and so on.

At first the Saxons, who were divided into numerous clans, waged only guerrilla warfare. Gradually, however, a Saxon chieftain named Witikind (or Widukind) succeeded in organizing the clans into an army capable of opposing the Franks in regular battle.

The first few years of conflict between the Franks and the Saxons ended with a Frankish victory in 777. Witikind fled to Denmark, where his brother-in-law was king. Most of the other Saxon chiefs surrendered to Charlemagne and accepted baptism.

To demonstrate his control over Saxony, Charlemagne held his next assembly at the Saxon capital of Paderborn. While there, he received an unusual embassy. Three dark-skinned men, dressed in silk robes and wearing turbans on their heads, rode into town. They were Muslims from Spain, and they wanted Charlemagne's help in overthrowing their caliph, or ruler. To help persuade Charlemagne, they said that the caliph was oppressing the Christians of northern Spain. They offered Charlemagne land and cities in exchange for his aid. And they promised that an army of

The Muslim embassy from Spain seeks Charlemagne's support in battle. He agreed to help them, but later regretted his decision.

Muslim rebels would join his forces in the Spanish city of Saragossa.

The idea of obtaining more territory while also championing Christianity appealed greatly to Charlemagne. So he agreed to invade Spain. It turned out to be one of the poorest decisions of his life.

# The Battle of Roncesvalles

Charlemagne set out for Spain in the spring of 778. He first approached the Christian city of Pamplona (or Pampeluna). To his surprise, he was greeted with hostility rather than welcome. Apparently the Christians were quite content with the caliph's rule and saw no reason to revolt against him. Charlemagne then made for the Muslim city of Saragossa, where he was supposed to join up with a Muslim rebel army. The army never appeared. It seems it had broken up when its general was assassinated.

At that point, Charlemagne received news that Witikind had returned to Saxony from Denmark and was at that moment preparing to attack Frankland. Reluctantly, Charlemagne gave his troops the order to withdraw, and the Franks headed back across the Pyrenees Mountains.

It was mid August when the Frankish army made its way through a narrow pass called Roncesvalles and descended into Frankland. Behind it, moving much more slowly, came the ox-drawn wagons that carried the army's supplies. A small rear guard accompanied the baggage train. Suddenly a boulder crashed down from the surrounding cliffs and hit one of the wagons. As the baggage train halted in surprise, a band of Basque guerrilla fighters (the Basques were native to the Pyrenees) fell on the rear

The fortress-city of Saragossa in the 1600s. In Charlemagne's time, Saragossa was noted for the excellent swords its blacksmiths produced. A typical sword was nearly three feet long and could be used for both thrusting and cutting.

guard. They killed every Frank in it. Then they seized the supplies and disappeared into the mountains.

Even though it was Charlemagne's first defeat, the engagement at Roncesvalles was a minor military incident. Yet it became immortalized through *The Song of Roland*, the most popular epic of the Middle Ages. The poem fired people's imaginations. In it, one of the Franks, Hroudland or Roland, is portrayed as a mighty warrior "who had conquered many lands for his aged white-haired uncle Charles [meaning Charlemagne, who was really only thirty-six at the time and no relation to Roland] and preferred to die fighting than to sound his horn for help." The poem is full of action and heroism. It is also inaccurate and exaggerated. For example, in it the Christian Basques have been transformed into Muslim Saracens, and an imaginary villain named Ganelon has been added to the plot.

Nevertheless, *The Song of Roland* was extremely important in medieval times. It showed how a king and his nobles were supposed to behave—with bravery, loyalty, and pride. It was the model for other romantic tales, including those about King Arthur and the knights of the Round Table. An early version of the poem was recited to William the Conqueror's troops when he successfully invaded England in 1066. The poem also inspired the crusaders who went to Palestine in the eleventh, twelfth, and thirteenth centuries to wrest the Holy Land from its Muslim rulers.

In addition to inspiring poems and legends, the death of Roland at Roncesvalles inspired many paintings. This French illumination was made in the 1400s.

# Wars and More Wars

Despite his glumness over the defeat at Roncesvalles and his failure to capture even a single Muslim city in Spain, Charlemagne soon plunged into new wars. Success in war was crucial for a medieval king. Conquered territory and plunder not only made him rich, it ensured the loyalty of his followers.

Charlemagne's most ferocious struggle was with his old enemies, the Saxons. In 782, Witikind again raised the banner of revolt. In the battle of Suntel Mountain, he succeeded in wiping out more than half of the Frankish army that had been sent to oppose him. Charlemagne rushed to the scene, only to find that—as in the past—Witikind and his followers had disappeared into the general population. Furious and frustrated, Charlemagne rounded up some 4,500 Saxons, including women and children, and had them all beheaded in a single day. The event became known as the Verden Massacre.

Determined to wipe out Saxon resistance, Charlemagne then began a reign of terror. First, he issued a series of harsh capitularies, or laws. They provided the death penalty for a long list of what were then considered offenses against Christianity. These included refusing to be baptized, eating meat during Lent, and cremating the dead. Second, he sent out Frankish troops to burn every Saxon village and field they could. Tens of thousands of Saxons starved to death during the summer of 784.

Charlemagne accepts the surrender of Witikind. The Saxon ruler was forced to convert to Christianity, and at his baptism Charlemagne served as godfather. Like all Saxons who converted to Christianity, Witikind swore to give up pagan gods, the devil, and the "devil's works and words."

Finally, in 785, Witikind agreed to surrender and accept baptism. Charlemagne showered him with gifts—and then issued new capitularies that required the Saxons to contribute 20 percent of their income to the Christian Church. It was a heavy burden for the impoverished Saxons, but they were too weak to protest.

Next Charlemagne turned his attention to Bavaria, which lay to the south of Saxony. Like the Saxons, the Bavarians were German, but unlike their northern neighbors, they were already Christian. In a series of diplomatic maneuvers backed by shows of force, Charlemagne succeeded in capturing Duke Tassilo, Bavaria's ruler (and incidentally Charlemagne's cousin). The duke and his family were sent to monastery and nunnery for the rest of their lives, and Bavaria became part of Frankland. All the Germanic peoples of mainland Europe were now united under a single monarch.

Charlemagne spent the years from 788 to 795 battling various

Slavic peoples to the east. He was not interested in taking over their territories. He just wanted to stop them from raiding his borders. As a result of these border wars, the Slavic peoples were allowed to retain their independence in exchange for paying tribute and promising to keep the peace.

During approximately the same period, Charlemagne fought a savage war against the Avars. These were a Mongolian people who had migrated from central Asia. Superb archers and horsemen, they still wore their black hair in long pigtails down their backs. They lived in a settlement known as the Ring, situated in what is now mostly Hungary. In the center of the Ring stood their ruler's palace. It was filled with gold coins, silver cups, jeweled swords, and other treasure the Avars had collected over more than two centuries of conquest. Surrounding the palace were nine concentric rings of land about twenty miles apart. Each ring was separated from its neighboring ring by high wooden walls covered with earth. Gates in the walls enabled people to pass from one ring to the next. Within each ring lay villages and farms.

It took the Franks seven years to defeat the Avars. Charlemagne was extremely generous with their treasure. Keeping only a small part for himself, he gave some to the pope, some to churches throughout Frankland, and some to his nobles. Unfortunately, the influx of so much wealth, combined with a scarcity of goods caused by the war, brought about a sharp rise in prices. As for the Avars, only a few survived. They moved away from the area of the Ring and were absorbed by other peoples. In fact, they disappeared so completely that many Slavs still have a saying, "To disappear like the Avars."

# Governing an Empire

By this time Charlemagne was in his early fifties. His fourth wife, Fastrada, whom he had married after the death of his beloved Hildegarde, had herself died, and he was contentedly married to his fifth wife, Liutgard.

Charlemagne also enjoyed his numerous children and grandchildren. They ate with him when he was at home and accompanied him when he traveled abroad. His favorite son, Charles, was being groomed to succeed him on the throne. His eldest son, Pepin the Hunchback, had been made overlord of Italy, and a third son, Louis, had been named overlord of Aquitaine. Nor were his daughters neglected. They received the same schooling as their brothers. In fact, Charlemagne was so devoted to his daughters that he refused to let them marry, even for diplomatic reasons. He did, however, allow them to have lovers.

As Charlemagne grew older, he became less harsh in his dealings with many of his enemies. For example, he pardoned Tassilo, the former ruler of Bavaria. When Pepin the Hunchback conspired to overthrow him, he imprisoned the prince in a monastery instead of executing him for treason. He did not insist that the Avars become Christians but left it up to them to decide whether they wanted to convert. When the Saxons revolted yet again, they

Charlemagne originally planned to divide his kingdom among his three sons. But the division never took place. Both Pepin and Charles died, leaving Louis as the sole heir.

were allowed to return to their old laws and traditions. If they violated any capitulary, they were fined rather than executed.

Charlemagne's age made it increasingly difficult for him to wage war every year. So instead he concentrated on governing his empire. He reviewed the system of uniform weights and measures and the system of uniform coinage that he had previously established. Early in his reign, he had started road- and bridge-building programs. Now he extended the roads and ordered construction of a great wooden bridge, the first to cross the Rhine River. The bridge took ten years to complete. The king also tried to have a canal dug that would connect the Rhine and Danube rivers, but he had to give up the project because of inadequate technology.

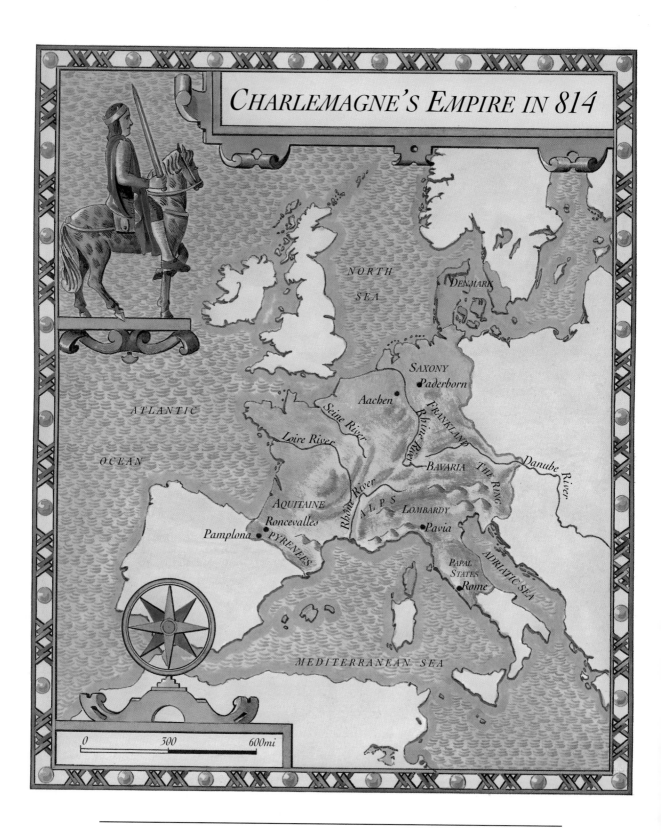

# CHARLEMAGNE'S EMPIRE IN 814

NORTH SEA

DENMARK

ATLANTIC

OCEAN

SAXONY

Paderborn

Aachen

FRANKLAND

Seine River

Loire River

Rhine River

BAVARIA

THE RING

Danube River

AQUITAINE

Rhône River

ALPS

LOMBARDY

Roncevalles

Pamplona

PYRENEES

Pavia

PAPAL STATES

Rome

ADRIATIC SEA

MEDITERRANEAN SEA

0    300    600mi

# The Rule of Law

Charlemagne spent considerable time issuing new capitularies. These covered all sorts of topics, from incorrect grammar and choral singing in church to road tolls and murder. Because many men had become priests to avoid serving in the army, he decreed that no one could do so without his permission. The only way to avoid military service was by paying a large tax. Charlemagne also ordered his subjects to provide food and lodging to pilgrims. And he forbade anyone from taking advantage of orphans, widows, or foreigners.

Perhaps the most unusual thing about the capitularies was the fact that they were set down in writing. That made them more precise than oral rules and thus a good tool for governing a large area.

To help enforce his capitularies, Charlemagne employed a system of *missi dominici*, or royal emissaries. They were sent out in pairs, one layman and one churchman. They read the capitularies out loud. They held court to make certain the laws were being obeyed and to hear appeals from the people. They checked the financial records of landowning nobles and bishops, and even looked into the behavior of priests, monks, and nuns. Then they reported back to Charlemagne on the state of his kingdom. To ensure that the *missi* did not become corrupt or overly friendly with a local lord, the king often shifted them from one part of Frankland to another.

Charlemagne issued at least 113 collections of laws during his reign, of which 65 still survive.

# A Grand Capital

Yet another of Charlemagne's accomplishments was the construction of a permanent capital. For its site the king chose the small town of Aachen (called Aix-la-Chapelle by the French). It lay near some medicinal springs in the rolling hill country of what is now western Germany.

The two main structures at Aachen were a chapel and a palace. The chapel, known as the Basilica of Saint Mary the Virgin, was eight-sided, with a lead-covered dome on top. The doors were

Charlemagne was very proud of the chapel he had built at Aachen. Some years later, it was damaged by an earthquake but was rebuilt. Eventually, it was destroyed by bombs during World War II.

bronze, and the interior was decorated with marble columns and mosaics that the pope had sent to Charlemagne. The king attended services as often as four times a day.

From the chapel, a covered walkway led up the hill to the marble-and-stone palace. Its rooms included an armory, or weapons room, a library, a treasury, and a wardrobe room. There was also a marble swimming pool large enough for one hundred swimmers to use at a time. A great bronze eagle with widespread wings perched on top of the roof. Attached to the palace was a building used entirely for government business. Around the palace stretched an immense park stocked with deer, wild boar, and other animals, where Charlemagne, his family, and his nobles could hunt.

Charlemagne was eager to improve education in his kingdom. Accordingly, an important feature of the palace was a school, run by a church scholar from England named Alcuin. Although designed mostly for the royal family, the school was open to anyone interested in learning. Students and scholars were recruited from all over Frankland. Alcuin wrote textbooks on such subjects as grammar and spelling. He also trained teachers. One result of his efforts was the increasing use of a new, easier-to-read script called Carolingian* minuscule. Our modern printing and writing developed from this new script.

Within the palace was a sort of academy, attended by

---

*Carolingian* is the name of the dynasty, or ruling family, to which Charlemagne belonged. The Carolingians were a family of Frankish kings who ruled from the mid 700s to 987. Charlemagne, his father Pepin the Short, and Pepin's father, Charles Martel, who founded the dynasty, were the most important Frankish rulers. The name *Carolingian* is often used to describe the people and events of that period of time.

Carolingian minuscule was not only easier to read but also more attractive than the Roman script that people had previously used. Roman script, called majuscule, consisted entirely of capital letters.

Charlemagne and many of his courtiers. They listened to lectures, wrote poetry, and discussed such subjects as theology, and Greek and Roman literature. They called one another by biblical or classical names. Charlemagne, for example, was known as David, after the biblical Jewish king.

## The Position of the Jews

Many of Charlemagne's predecessors had tried to force their Jewish subjects to convert to Christianity. Charlemagne, on the other hand, practiced tolerance. He allowed Jews to own land and to follow their religion without interference. He also encouraged them to pursue various commercial activities, especially foreign trade. Jewish merchants exported grain, wine, and gold to the Arab and Byzantine

Empires. They imported spices, medicines, and textiles, giving Charlemagne first choice of these items in return for his protection.

In 797 Charlemagne sent a Jew named Isaac of Aachen as interpreter for a pair of Frankish envoys to the court of Harun al-Rashid, the ruler of the Arab Empire. The envoys died during the trip. Isaac, however, returned safely to Aachen five years later. His arrival caused a sensation, for he was accompanied by something that had not been seen in Europe for almost a thousand years: an elephant. The animal, which was named Abu'l Abbas, accompanied Charlemagne on his travels and became a major tourist attraction for people visiting Aachen.

# The Pope and the Emperor

Charlemagne had always regarded himself as a Christian king. This meant converting as many pagans as possible to Christianity. Christian kingship also meant repairing and beautifying church buildings, introducing the Gregorian chant into church services, and educating the clergy. A Christian king also was not shy about giving opinions on theological questions, such as what role icons and relics should play in Christian worship.

In 795 Pope Hadrian died and was succeeded by the controversial Leo III. His opponents accused him of having bought his office. They also accused him of immorality and perjury. In 799 a group of them pulled him off his horse, beat him savagely, and dragged him off to a monastery to die. He managed to escape. But when he appealed to Charlemagne for help, the king—instead of traveling to Rome—told the pope to come to Paderborn. It was clear who depended on whom.

Leo III remained in Paderborn for three months, during which time Charlemagne investigated the charges against him. Apparently they were true. But Charlemagne felt it was more important to maintain the spiritual authority of the papacy than to punish the pope. Accordingly, he sent Leo III back to Rome, together with a troop of Frankish soldiers to protect him.

Charlemagne, shown here at his coronation as emperor, stood six and one-half feet tall. A strong, vigorous man, he exercised every day and ate and drank in moderation. Surprisingly, he had a rather high-pitched voice.

Yet even though Leo III was restored to the papal throne, the Romans still muttered and complained about him. So the following year Charlemagne decided to go to Rome himself. Accompanied by a large army and his entire court, he entered the city on November 24, 800. There he called for a public trial of the pope. After three weeks, the jury of churchmen and nobles could not reach a verdict. The only solution was for the pope to swear that he was innocent in public, before God and Saint Peter. Leo III did so on December 23, and the matter was closed.

Two days later was Christmas Day. Rome's Saint Peter's Cathedral was decorated with green branches and purple tapestries. A cross composed of hundreds of candles glowed above the altar. Thousands of people from all parts of Frankland crowded the church.

At the request of Leo III, Charlemagne had put aside his usual clothes for the tunic, robe, and sandals of a Roman noble. As he knelt before the pope during mass, Leo III suddenly stepped forward and placed a gold crown on the king's head. The onlookers, seemingly well rehearsed, shouted three times, "To Charles, Augustus, crowned by God, great and peaceful emperor, life and victory." The pope then knelt and bowed his head three times to Charlemagne.

The king of the Franks was now head of the Roman Empire in the West, the first such ruler in more than three hundred years. Since the empire was held together more by Christianity than by language, law, or government, it later became known as the Holy Roman Empire. In one form or another, it lasted until the 1800s.

Historians have long argued about Charlemagne's coronation. Some say he knew about it beforehand, while others disagree. Some argue that the coronation indicated the pope was superior to the emperor, because Leo III had crowned Charlemagne instead of simply anointing him. In other words, the crown was the pope's to give. Other historians assert the opposite. Because Charlemagne decreed that the emperor's consent would be required to elect future popes, the emperor was clearly superior to the pope. The issue was one that would trouble Europe for many centuries to come.

In any event, Charlemagne began to act like an emperor. He ordered the Romans to swear allegiance to him and agree to live under his rule. He had new coins struck with the words "renewal of the Roman Empire" on them. And he eventually signed a treaty with the Byzantine Empire, the Roman Empire of the East, that acknowledged his new status.

# The Final Years

The years after his coronation brought new problems and sorrows into Charlemagne's life. His wife Liutgard had died early in 800. In 804 the Saxons rebelled once again. This time Charlemagne ordered them removed from Saxony and resettled in distant parts of the empire. There was widespread famine in 807, and thousands of starving peasants roamed the land, begging and looting.

In 808 a new enemy appeared: the Northmen, or Vikings, of Scandinavia. Sailing their black, dragon-prowed ships along the coast, they carried out a series of devastating raids on Frankish settlements. Although the Northmen stopped raiding when their king died, Charlemagne realized the attacks were bound to resume. Accordingly, he ordered the Franks to build a navy, even though they had almost no experience fighting at sea.

The years 810 and 811 were even worse. First the elephant Abu'l Abbas died and was sincerely mourned. Then a plague swept through the empire, killing thousands of people, including Charlemagne's favorite daughter and his son Pepin. The plague was followed by an outbreak of cattle and horse disease that wiped out many of the animals needed for food and for the transport of military supplies. Lastly, Charlemagne's favorite son, Charles, who was supposed to succeed his father on the throne, also died, apparently of a stroke. Charlemagne had hoped to divide his empire into three smaller kingdoms that would cooperate with one another. Now only his youngest legitimate son, Louis, remained to inherit.

Accordingly, Charlemagne summoned Louis to Aachen. In September 813, he called a national assembly and asked it to elect Louis as co-emperor. On September 11, inside the church Charlemagne had built, he placed a gold crown on his son's head.

By this time, Charlemagne had made out his will. He left only one-twelfth of his treasure to members of his family. Small amounts were earmarked as alms for the poor and gifts to palace servants. Almost all the rest went to the empire's twenty-one archbishops.

Charlemagne had become increasingly devout over the past few years. He spent much of his time writing sermons to be read to the people. He worked on a new text of the four Gospels. He even thought of abdicating, or stepping down from the throne, and becoming a monk.

In January 814, Charlemagne fell ill with one of his recurrent fevers. As usual, he tried to cure himself by fasting. But the fever turned into a lung inflammation, and on January 28, at the advanced age of seventy-two, Charlemagne died. He was buried in the chapel at Aachen.

The empire Charlemagne created survived without change for only a few decades after his death. But many of the ideas and institutions of his reign lasted for hundreds of years. For example, the idea of a king who is both the spiritual and the political head of his nation remained popular until recently. The Christian culture he had done so much to strengthen flourished all through the Middle Ages and still plays a major role in world affairs. The descendants of his nobles influenced how the nations of western Europe developed. As one historian explains, this ruling elite led European

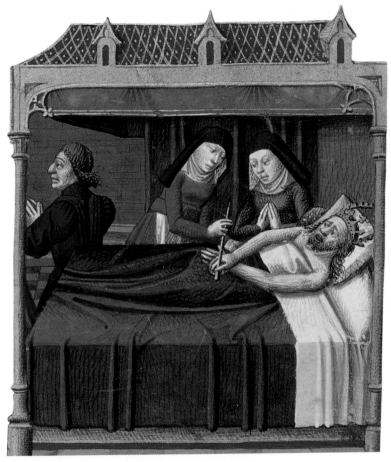

**Charlemagne was greatly mourned after his death. Some people even revered him as a saint.**

nations "to develop along common paths. They may have spoken different languages and worn different costumes, but they observed common principles of government, religion, and commerce." Even Europe's population patterns were influenced by Charlemagne. As a result of his conquests, areas that had been uninhabited since the fall of Rome became populated once again. Is it any wonder that many historians call him the "father of Europe"?

# PART TWO

In addition to performing military and administrative tasks, Charlemagne's courtiers enjoyed such entertainments as listening to music, especially old Frankish ballads.

# Everyday Life in the Time of Charlemagne

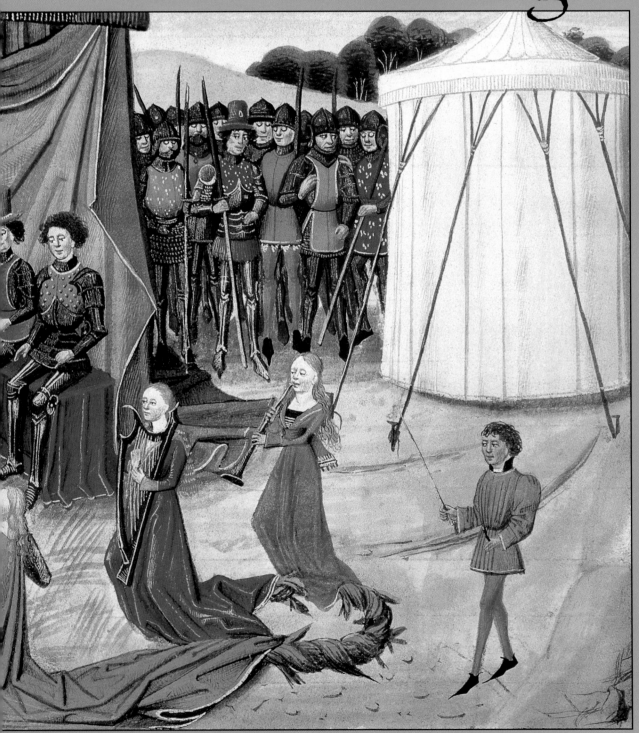

# The Christian Church

The basic unit of church organization was the diocese. It was headed by a bishop, whose church was known as a cathedral. Bishops were appointed by Charlemagne and were usually nobles. Once, when Charlemagne wanted to appoint a man of low rank as bishop, all his officials objected. Even Queen Hildegarde tried to persuade her husband to choose an aristocrat for the position.

Bishops generally lived a life of luxury similar to that of lay nobles. They inhabited comfortable palaces, often dressed in silk clothing, gave elaborate dinners, and enjoyed drinking and hunting. At the same time, they did not neglect their religious and civic duties. Bishops were responsible for training future priests. Some bishops became *missi.* Others took part in military expeditions, either raising a certain number of soldiers from the workers on their estates or actually joining in the fighting. A council of bishops decided such matters as who the true prophets were and which religious practices people should follow.

In turn, dioceses were divided into parishes, each with its own church. In the beginning, these had been located mostly in cities and towns. During the 600s, the situation began to change as a few rural churches were built. Charlemagne greatly speeded up the change. Formerly, the Christian Church had been supported

The sacrament of baptism welcomed people into the Christian Church.

by the large amount of land that it owned. In addition, some individuals had voluntarily tithed, or given the Church one-tenth of their income. Charlemagne made tithing compulsory. Now the Church had a large and steady source of revenue. The result was the construction of hundreds of rural churches led by parish priests. The priests usually came from peasant stock and could neither read nor write. But they had close ties with their congregations and ministered effectively to them. Many priests were married.

A parish priest was supposed to know enough Latin to recite prayers correctly. He had to be able to chant hymns "not with a voice too loud or disordered . . . but in an even and rounded voice." He was responsible for performing such rituals as baptism, marriage, and burial. He was also responsible for collecting tithes.

Priests taught their congregations mostly by preaching. Sermons dealt with behavior as well as with basic Christian beliefs. People were urged to be kind, modest, and charitable. They were not supposed to eat or drink too much. They were to spend Sundays attending church services instead of working.

Babies were commonly baptized on Easter eve or on Pentecost, the seventh Sunday after Easter. Boys from aristocratic families usually received their grandfather's name. Some parents chose Christian names for their children, such as Benedictus or Clementia. Other parents preferred names from the Old Testament, such as Benjamin, David, and Samuel.

The typical age at which people married depended on their rank. Nobles married at a younger age than peasants. Prospective marriages were announced in the parish church for three Sundays in succession. This was known as reading the banns. The parish priest performed the marriage at the door to the church, after which a nuptial mass was held inside. This was followed by various celebrations, the most common of which was a feast. Another custom was for people to form a line and dance around the church singing at the top of their lungs.

Kings and high church officials were buried inside a church. Well-to-do people gave gifts to their local church so they might be buried in its courtyard. Everyone else was buried in the parish cemetery. In their wills, people often asked their descendants to pray for them after they died. They also had their names engraved on the stones of their church's altar so they would be remembered.

Carolingian churches were usually made of wood, although some, especially cathedrals, were built of stone. The stones were sometimes quarried, but most came from the ruins of Roman buildings and monuments. Roofs were covered either with wooden shingles or with lead.

Cathedrals in particular were highly decorated. Windows were made of colored glass. Doors were cast from bronze. Marble mosaics covered the floors. Wall paintings had to follow a set code. For example, the painting of a noble had to show him carrying his weapons. The painting of an apostle had to show his attributes. Thus, Peter was bald, while Matthew had a beard.

Saint George's church, in present-day Germany, was built in the tenth century and is a fine example of Carolingian architecture.

Until Charlemagne, churches had only a single tower. During his reign they often had several, including a watchtower for defense and a bell tower to house the bells that called the faithful to prayer. The royal chapel at Aachen boasted identical towers on either side of the entrance. They added greatly to the chapel's impressive appearance.

Religious feasts punctuated the Carolingian year. Saint Martin's Day marked the beginning of winter. Spring opened with the great week of Easter. Saint John's Day signaled the start of summer. Saint Remi's Day meant the harvest time of fall. And there were, of course, fifty-two Sundays a year.

In addition, as churches obtained the relics of saints, many more religious holidays were added to the calendar. Relics were believed to protect people against such ills as disease, poverty, and enemy attacks. The demand for relics was so great, in fact, that some were stolen from one church and brought to another. Such thievery was considered "a pious action inspired by God."

# Life in a Monastery

One of the most important religious developments of the Carolingian period was the monastic movement. During the early years of Christianity, many people in Palestine and Egypt had abandoned city life to live in the desert or the mountains. They believed this was the only way to escape the corrupt material world to become truly religious. Most of these individuals became hermits. A few lived in small groups in monasteries.

As Christianity spread across Europe, becoming a hermit fell out of favor. Cold weather, thieves, and wild animals made living alone too dangerous. Then, too, church leaders believed that you could better achieve holiness in a community than you could by yourself. Accordingly, they encouraged the establishment of monasteries.

By Charlemagne's time, there were many monasteries in western Europe. These were often run according to a set of rules called the Rule of Saint Benedict, or the Benedictine Rule. These regulations for monastic life had been laid down in 529 by Saint Benedict, an Italian monk. Benedict believed the only important thing in life was serving God. Monks were supposed to spend their lives within the monastery and not wander about. They were required to swear a threefold vow of poverty, chastity, and obedience. Poverty meant giving up all worldly goods—land, money, and personal property. Chastity meant not marrying or having relationships

Saint Benedict was a hermit for several years before founding a monastery at Monte Cassino, Italy.

with women. Obedience meant obeying the abbot, or monastery head. "Let no one in the monastery follow the will of his own heart."

A monk's daily life combined prayer, hard work, and study. Each day he participated in seven ceremonial rites, called offices. At midnight a monk rose from his bed to sing the first office of Matins and Lauds. Then he went back to bed until the second office of Prime at sunrise. The third office of Terce and Mass was followed by a meeting in the chapter house at which the monks discussed monastery business.

After the meeting, monks went their separate ways. Some toiled in the fields, growing grain and vegetables for food and grapes for wine. Some cultivated herbs for making medicines or cared for the monastery's geese and poultry. Monks with special skills worked as carpenters and masons. Educated monks copied manuscripts. Others received free time each day to study the Bible. Everyone took his turn cleaning oil lamps, scouring pots, and sweeping the floor. According to the Benedictine Rule, idleness was "the enemy of the soul."

The fourth office of the day, Sext, was followed by High Mass. Then came dinner, which was served at noon. Like all meals, it was eaten in silence. The only sound was the voice of the monk who was reading the holy lesson of the day. After the fifth office, Nones, came several more hours of work and study. Then a short rest before the office of Vespers, supper, the office of Compline, and so to bed.

Monks provided people who lived nearby with many services. They distributed food and clothing to the poor. They ran orphanages and hospitals. They took in travelers overnight. They cleared forests and drained swamps. Perhaps most important of all, they kept records of events in their community and maintained libraries and schools.

The monastic movement included some women, who lived a life similar to that of monks. Nuns, however, often relied on servants to do the heavy physical work while they concentrated on copying manuscripts, caring for the sick, and doing needlework on altar cloths. The head of a nunnery was called an abbess. There was also a male chaplain to conduct mass for the nuns and to hear their confessions. Because nunneries demanded a dowry, the nuns of Charlemagne's time all came from noble families.

# Education

At first, the only schools in Charlemagne's empire were monastic schools. These were limited to members of the clergy. Students learned to read the Bible and to do simple arithmetic. Some of them became scribes and copied the writings of ancient Rome, producing the manuscripts that kept learning alive in the early Middle Ages.

Scribes made their own writing materials. To make parchment, you began by taking the skin of a calf, goat, or sheep and soaking it in lime. Next, you stretched the skin and scraped it free of hair. Finally, you cut it into sheets. You wrote with a quill pen, which you dipped into an inkhorn containing gall-iron ink, made from a soluble iron salt. You sat on a bench with your feet on a stool and wrote on top of a writing desk. Sometimes you copied a manuscript. Sometimes a reader dictated words to you. Many scribes made

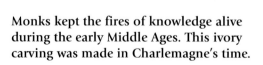

**Monks kept the fires of knowledge alive during the early Middle Ages. This ivory carving was made in Charlemagne's time.**

comments in the margins: "It is cold today." "How hairy this parchment is!"

Because it took so long to produce manuscripts, they were considered prized possessions. Readers were urged to "turn the pages gently, wash your hands, hold the book so, and lay something between it and your dress."

Gradually, cathedral schools developed. As their name implies, they were attached to a cathedral and were run by the bishop. Unlike monastic schools, they were open to lay students as well as clergy members. Girls, however, could not attend.

The curriculum, which was developed by Alcuin, was known as the liberal arts curriculum because it resembled the curriculum that *liberi*, or free men, had studied in ancient Rome. The curriculum was divided into two parts. There were three subjects having to do with letters: grammar, which meant the study of Latin; logic, or clear thinking; and rhetoric, or effective speech and writing. There were also four subjects having to do with numbers: arithmetic, astronomy, geometry, and music. All the liberal arts were considered "stepping stones" to the highest study of all, namely, the Bible.

Instruction in a cathedral school was usually in Latin. The teacher would read from a classical text and then explain what it meant. Because most students could not afford books, they relied on memory. They listened to the same lecture over and over so they would be sure to remember its main points.

For arithmetic and geometry, the Carolingians used Roman numerals, which did not include zero. The Arabic numbering system (which actually came from India) had not yet been introduced into western Europe.

# Life on a Manor

Most Carolingians were farmers. About three out of four were tenants who lived and worked on estates called manors.

In the center of a manor stood a group of buildings protected either by a hedge of trees or by a high wooden fence. The largest building was the manor house, which was usually made of stone. Its three or four rooms faced an inner court where one found a kitchen, a bakehouse, stables, barns, workshops, and possibly a mill. The manor house was inhabited either by the lord who owned the manor or by his steward.

Nearby stood the cottages of the farmers. These usually contained only one room. The framework was made of wooden beams, while the space between them was filled with a mixture of straw and clay. The roof was thatched with straw. A hole in the roof allowed smoke from the hearth to escape. The floor consisted of packed earth. Attached to each cottage was a garden, some farmland, and perhaps a vineyard.

Surrounding the central area were the manor's fields for growing crops and the pastures where animals grazed. Then came the woodlands. These furnished fuel for heating and cooking, timber for building, and birds and animals for food.

Farmers rented their land from the lord of the manor by providing services. In general, they had to spend three days a week plowing the manor's fields, gathering fruit, harvesting grain,

Carolingian peasants boil saltwater in order to obtain salt.

repairing buildings, cutting down trees, and doing anything else the lord required. The rest of the time, they were free to work their own land.

In addition to services, farmers had to pay certain fees to the lord. For example, they might bring in a load of wood in return for being permitted to gather firewood in the manor's woodlands. They might trade a hogshead of wine for the right to turn their pigs into the woodlands to feed on acorns, beechnuts, and berries. They might contribute one sheep every three years for the right to graze their animals on the manor's pastures.

Farmers who rented their land were known as serfs. The lord of the manor was supposed to protect them against attacks by robbers or foreign enemies. For their part, serfs were restricted in their daily lives. For example, they needed the lord's permission to leave the manor or to marry someone from another manor. On the other hand, no one could take away a serf's land so long as he provided the labor, food, and other services that were expected of him. There were also slaves on some manors, but their number was gradually decreasing.

The one out of four farmers who owned their land outright were known as freeholders. Instead of being situated on a manor, their cottages formed a village. A village's fields, pastures, and woodlands were owned and used by its freeholders in common.

# An Agricultural Revolution

Many manors and villages used a three-field system of farming in which they rotated their crops. One field grew spring crops (generally vegetables), which were planted in spring and harvested in the fall. A second field grew winter crops (mostly cereals). These were planted in the fall and harvested the following spring. The third field was left fallow, or unplanted. The next year, the field that had grown spring crops was left fallow. The field that had grown winter crops was planted with spring crops, and the fallow field was planted with winter crops, and so on. The system kept the soil from wearing out. This was important because the farmers did not use fertilizers. Also, the three-field system produced more crops than the ancient two-field system that kept half of the land fallow.

Farmers in Charlemagne's day made use of a new device that had apparently been invented in Asia. It was the padded horse collar.

In the past, the only way to harness a horse was with the throat-and-girth harness, which went around the animal's neck and stomach. Its disadvantage was that it tended to choke the horse when the animal pulled against it. The padded horse collar, in contrast, went around the horse's chest. This enabled the animal to pull at least three times the weight it could pull with the old harness.

Because they could move faster and work for longer hours than oxen, horses gradually began to replace oxen as plow animals. Nevertheless, many peasants continued using oxen. They were cheaper to feed than horses and, when they were no longer useful, were also good to eat.

Still another aid to agriculture that became popular under Charlemagne was the water mill, which was used to grind grain. Water mills were commonly found only on large manors. They were expensive to build and also called for a variety of skills. You needed to dam a running stream. You had to cut millstones, transport them from the quarry to the mill site, and set them in place. You needed a carpenter and a blacksmith to build the driving machinery. And of course you had to keep the mill in good condition. But mills saved so much labor that farmers willingly paid a percentage of their grain or flour to use them. As a result, mill owners were able to make a large profit.

Despite these aids, growing enough food was always a problem. Famine was common. As one historian explains, "Shortages could be caused by floods which delayed the sowing, winters which lasted too long, late frosts which destroyed the first crops, torrid summers which dried up the vegetation, and even an invasion of grasshoppers." When these occurred, people were reduced to killing their horses for food or eating earth mixed with a little flour. Some even became cannibals.

# Military Matters

Charlemagne's army consisted partly of cavalry, or men on horseback, and partly of infantry, or foot soldiers. In those days, soldiers had to provide their own equipment. Both cavalrymen (commonly known as knights) and infantrymen carried a round shield, a lance, a bow, two bowstrings, and twelve arrows. In addition, foot soldiers were armed with a dagger and a single-bladed battle axe. They often used the axe as a missile, hurling it at an enemy before engaging in hand-to-hand combat. Knights were further armed with a double-edged sword and a mace, or heavy club, that usually took the form of an iron ball covered with spikes. Fighting bishops liked the mace because they were not supposed to use a sword to shed blood.

Foot soldiers wore leather jackets for protection. On their heads, they sometimes

**A Carolingian foot soldier with his lance and shield**

wore caps reinforced with iron bands. Knights were dressed in a mail coat made of interlocking iron rings. A helmet made of either iron or boiled leather protected their heads.

In addition to providing their own equipment, knights had to provide their own horses. But a horse strong enough to carry a man in a mail coat was expensive. Indeed, such an animal cost as much as a farm! As a result, by Charlemagne's time the custom had developed of giving a man land as advance payment for service in the cavalry.

Charlemagne usually planned his military campaigns a year in advance. He studied maps of the enemy countryside and listened to the reports of spies. In general, campaigns began in May or June and lasted over the summer. In a few instances, particularly when besieging a town, it was necessary to remain on a battlefield through the winter.

Charlemagne favored an unusual battle strategy. Instead of keeping his troops together, he would divide his army into several columns, each of which crossed the frontier at a different place. This so confused his enemies, who did not know where the main blow would strike, that they usually began retreating. Then, at the crucial moment, Charlemagne would reunite his forces and make a decisive, successful attack.

# A Variety of Crafts

Blacksmiths were among the rarest artisans of Carolingian times, yet they were probably the most important. Without them, both warfare and agriculture would have been very different.

Blacksmiths made swords out of iron that they strengthened by adding a small amount of carbon. They welded the edges separately, and then shaped the sword with a file or whetstone. Such a sword was expensive; it cost as much as three cows! It was also considered the best sword made in Europe. Many knights gave their swords names. Charlemagne called his sword *Joyeuse*, or "joyful."

Blacksmiths made horseshoes and nails as well as farming tools. They also made tools used by other craftsmen, such as the carpenter's lathe. Because of the sparks that came from their forges, they were sometimes believed to be sorcerers or magicians. People would ask them "to cast or break spells . . . [and] to repair broken bones."

Goldsmiths started out with slabs of the precious metal, which they reduced to thin leaves by beating. Then they melted the leaves and used the liquid to gild copper and iron, and to write on parchment, glass, and marble. They made book bindings and altar pieces out of gold, and set jewels in a gold framework.

Making clothes was woman's work. Women were responsible for every step of the process. If the garment was made of linen, they

A blacksmith's skills were among the most highly valued in the early Middle Ages.

first cut a fibrous plant called flax. Then they shook out the seeds, soaked the flax in water, pounded it to remove the bark, and separated the fibers. If the garment was made of wool, they began by shearing the sheep. Then they washed and combed the wool.

Women carried spindles in their hands at all times, even when cooking meals or minding the children. It took several hand-spinners to make thread for one weaver. Weavers worked either in the home or in workshops on large estates. In the summer, they sometimes set up their looms outdoors.

# Food

Nobles and peasants alike lived mostly on bread, peas, and beans. The bread was made from barley, wheat, rye, or oats. The peas and beans were usually served in the form of porridge. Additional vegetables, usually made into soup, included beets, cabbage, carrots, leeks, onions, and turnips. Apples and grapes were the most popular fruits. Cow's milk was turned into butter and cheese. Some families raised chickens for eggs, which were often pickled so they would keep over the winter.

Meat was a luxury. Cattle, sheep, and pigs were slaughtered in late fall and salted to prevent decay. If served in stews, a single animal provided enough meat to last a peasant family the entire winter. In many places, people ate fish caught in the local fishpond or river. Nobles brought meat in from the hunt, especially deer and wild boar.

On Christmas Day, it was customary for the lord of the manor to throw a feast for his peasants. The main course usually consisted of a whole pig roasted on a spit.

People sweetened their food and drink with honey. Those who could afford it drank wine. Everyone else drank beer. Cider, made either from pears or wild apples, was also available. And if the grape and grain harvests were poor, people drank water. As one clergyman wrote: "Let us make use of a healthy, natural drink which will sometimes be of benefit to both body and soul—if it is drawn not from a muddy cistern [water tank] but from a clear well or the current of a transparent brook."

The Carolingians seasoned their food heavily with spices. Most prized were cinnamon, cloves, cumin, and pepper, which were imported from Asia.

# Clothing

Frankish men wore a shirt and pants made of linen, with a linen tunic on top. They wrapped narrow strips of cloth around their legs and thrust their feet into heavy leather or wooden shoes. In the winter they added a vest made of sheepskin if the man was a peasant, or fur if the man was a noble. The most common furs were beaver, marten, mole, and otter.

Noblemen also added a woolen cloak, either white or blue. It was shaped like a double square, fastened at both shoulders, and was so arranged that it came down almost to the ground in front and back but fell only to the knees at the sides. For a brief time, nobles adopted the short embroidered cloak worn by the neighboring Gauls. But Charlemagne objected. "What is the use of these little napkins?" he is supposed to have said. "I can't cover myself with them in bed. When I am on horseback I can't protect myself from the winds and the rain. When I go off to empty my bowels, I catch cold because my backside is frozen."

Carolingian nobles also liked to wear silk and brocade for special occasions. Charlemagne, too, dressed in finery on feast days, when he wore clothes interwoven with gold and shoes decorated with jewels.

Monks dressed much like peasants. The only difference was that instead of a tunic, they wore a long black robe with a hood.

Peasant women wore a single garment of coarse linen tied

From this manuscript illustration, we can get a sense of the way members of the nobility and Church dressed.

around the waist. Noblewomen wore a fine linen tunic with large sleeves, over which they threw a mantle. They fastened the tunic with a jeweled belt and used a jeweled headdress to hold their veils. Nuns likewise dressed in long tunics and covered their heads with a veil.

# Furniture

Furniture in Charlemagne's day was very simple. Families—both adults and children—slept together in one bed. Under the bed was a bottle of holy water to keep away the devil. A cradle usually stood close at hand so that the mother could rock it from the bed. Peasants covered themselves with animal skins. Nobles used linen sheets and down comforters. People stored their clothes and other belongings in wooden chests.

Most homes had either wooden benches or chairs with backs. Some monasteries placed down cushions on their chairs. They also covered their wooden tables with colored cloths.

Kitchens were equipped with a hearth, surrounded by andirons, chains, and pothooks. There were large kettles made of iron and leather for cooking stews. Plates were made of lead; pots of iron, lead, tin, or wood. Tableware was usually made of wood.

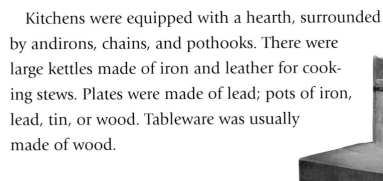

**Charlemagne sat on this marble throne in his palace at Aachen.**

# Health and Medical Care

Many people did not live long in the early Middle Ages. This was particularly true of infants. About one out of three died within two weeks after birth. In addition, many people practiced infanticide as a way of limiting their families. In most cases, they did not actually kill babies; they just "forgot" to feed them. This was particularly true of female babies.

Many adults died before they reached their fifties. One reason was that they seldom bathed. (The only exceptions were monks, who bathed once a week, and Charlemagne, who supposedly took a bath every day.) Their bodies were covered with lice and fleas, making them very susceptible to disease. In addition, their diet was high in starch and carbohydrates but low in protein. This also lowered their resistance. With so much fighting going on, battle wounds were common. So were broken bones caused by poor farming tools.

Nevertheless, physicians did their best. They prescribed a tree product called balsam for coughs and an ointment that combined chicken fat, wormwood, laurel berries, and oil of roses for asthma. Wounds were cleaned with honey or wine. If they became gangrenous, physicians would amputate the affected limb or area. Because there were no anesthetics, the patient was dulled with a heavy slug of wine and, if necessary, held down by force.

Physicians smeared burns with butter and egg whites. A mixture of vinegar, oil, and sulphur was recommended for toothache. Fasting was recommended for stomach troubles and for good health in general. People who suffered from inflamed eyes were told to bathe them in a solution of herbs and wine.

Physicians always asked patients under what star they had been born. Certain herbs and other remedies went with certain planets. You could take medicine only if the moon was in a favorable position. There were lucky and unlucky days for letting blood, as well.

Many people preferred to rely on Christian faith rather than a physician for cures. They would go to a cathedral and pray to the Virgin Mary or touch the relic of a saint and ask for help. Some drank holy oil to drive out the demons they believed had made them ill.

# Fairs and Other Entertainments

A highlight of the year for peasants was the great fair held at one of several cities. Merchants would set up their booths in a large meadow. The meadow was enclosed by a gated fence, and the merchants had to pay a toll to enter the area. Sometimes a merchant would try to avoid the toll by burrowing under the fence or climbing over it. Most fairs lasted a week, but the one held at the Abbey of Saint Denis outside Paris lasted an entire month.

It was great fun to wander along the rows of booths. There were local goods, such as wine, honey, and cloth. There were cheeses and salted meats and dyes for coloring fabric. There were also exotic goods from faraway lands, "purple and silken robes with orange borders, stamped leather jerkins [old-style jackets], peacock's feathers, and the scarlet plumage of flamingos . . . scents and pearls and spices, almonds and raisins, and monkeys for [the wives of Frankish nobles] to play with."

One could hear many different languages and dialects at a fair, for people came from all parts of Charlemagne's empire, as well as from England and Ireland. There was also entertainment. Jugglers tossed balls into the air. Conjurers swallowed fire or swords. Minstrels sang sweet songs. There were men with performing bears, and tumblers who rolled across the grass and twisted their bodies into various shapes.

Sundays and saints' days were another source of fun. Then peasants were exempted from all work except "carrying for the army, carrying food, or carrying [if need be] the body of a lord to its grave." After attending services in the parish church, the peasants would gather in the churchyard to sing and dance. Many of the songs were pagan songs or love songs, neither of which were approved of by the Church. The Church also frowned on people riding on wooden horses and on women dancing in a circle. But the objections of parish priests, and even of bishops, had no effect. Peasants continued to sing and dance the way their ancestors had.

# PART THREE

A page from a manuscript
made in Carolingian times.
Carolingians stored their
books in one of three ways:
in a chest, lying flat, or on a
shelf that sloped to one side.

# The Carolingians in
## Their Own Words

One of the most famous monasteries of the Carolingian period was the monastery of Reichenau, in what is now Switzerland. The following poem was written by one of the monks who lived and studied there:

### PANGUR BAN

I and Pangur Ban my cat
'Tis a like task we are at:
Hunting mice is his delight,
Hunting words I sit all night.

Better far than praise of men
'Tis to sit with book and pen;
Pangur bears me no ill will,
He too plies his simple skill.

'Tis a merry thing to see
At our tasks how glad are we,
When at home we sit and find
Entertainment to our mind.

Oftentimes a mouse will stray
In the hero Pangur's way;
Oftentimes my keen thought set
Takes a meaning in its net.

'Gainst the wall he sets his eye
Full and fierce and sharp and sly;
'Gainst the wall of knowledge I
All my little wisdom try.

When a mouse darts from its den
O how glad is Pangur then!
O what gladness do I prove
When I solve the doubts I love!

So in peace our tasks we ply,
Pangur Ban, my cat and I;
In our arts we find our bliss,
I have mine and he has his.

Practice every day has made
Pangur perfect in his trade;
I get wisdom day and night
Turning darkness into light.

Monks spent hours and hours "turning darkness into light." This letter *Q* decorated a medieval manuscript.

Many monasteries sent out missionaries to non-Christian parts of Europe to try to convert the population. The missionaries were not always well received, as the following account by Alcuin shows:

## MISSIONARIES AND MARTYRS

*Two priests followed . . . [Bishop Willibrord's] example, burning with intense fervour for the Faith, and both of them were called by the same name of Hewald. Their mission in life was the same; identical were their deaths. One was fair, the other dark, the only difference being the colour of their hair; but dark Hewald was keener on learning than the fair Hewald. They entered the land of the pagan Saxons, attempting to win some of them over to Christ. But when the wretches [the Saxons] saw the new morals and customs of the Faith, they were afraid that the cult of their ancient gods might be . . . [overthrown] rapidly and completely. Suddenly they laid hold of the monks and put them to a cruel death: fair Hewald was immediately murderously slaughtered but rugged dark Hewald, poor wretch, they long tortured, and tossed the corpses of both into the waters of the Rhine. The bodies were carried off in a wondrous way against that river's powerful current, floating eleven miles back to their companions. Wherever the bodies touched at night-time, a brilliant ray of light shone more brightly than the stars and the murderers of these holy men saw it gleaming on throughout the night. One of them appeared at night to a comrade of his, and said: "You can find the bodies without delay, where you see the light streaming from the heavens." Nor did this vision deceive the Hewalds' comrades, for they found the corpses in that very place and buried them with the honour that is due to holy martyrs.*

As tutor of Charlemagne's son Pepin, Alcuin used the technique of question and answer. The following questions by Pepin, with Alcuin's answers, deal with astronomy and geography:

P.: *What is the sun?*
A.: *The splendor of the world, the beauty of heaven, the grace of nature, the glory of the day, the distributor of the hours.*

P.: *What is the moon?*
A.: *The eye of night, the herald [announcer] of storms.*

P.: *What are the stars?*
A.: *The picture of the summit, the guides of sailors, the adornment of night.*

P.: *What is rain?*
A.: *The conception of the earth, the producer of crops.*

P.: *What is a cloud?*
A.: *The disturbance of the air, the mobility of water, the dryness of the land.*

P.: *What is the earth?*
A.: *The mother of growing things, the nurse of living things, the storeroom of life, the devourer of all things.*

P.: *What is the sea?*
A.: *The path of daring, the frontier of the land, the divider of regions, the home of rivers, the source of rain clouds.*

P.: *What is water?*
A.: *The support of life, the cleansing of sin.*

P.: *What is frost?*
A.: *The persecution of grass, the destroyer of leaves, the fetters [chains] of the land, the bridge of waters.*

P.: *What is snow?*
A.: *Dry water.*

P.: *What is winter?*
A.: *The exile of summer.*

P.: *What is spring?*
A.: *The painter of the earth.*

P.: *What is summer?*
A.: *The readornment of the land, the ripeness of the crops.*

P.: *What is autumn?*
A.: *The granary of the year.*

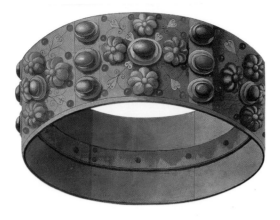

The iron strip inside the Iron Crown of Lombardy was supposedly made from one of the nails used to crucify Jesus. Charlemagne's successors wore this crown in honor of his victory over the Lombards in 774. Napoleon Bonaparte crowned himself emperor with it in 1804.

Revolts against Charlemagne broke out in 786 and again in 792. After putting them down, the king ordered all his free subjects to swear an oath of loyalty to him over the bones of a saint:

> *I promise that, from this day forward, I will be the most faithful man of the most pious Emperor, my lord Charles, son of King Pepin and Queen Bertha [Bertrada]; and I will be so in all sincerity, without deceit or ill-intention, for the honour of his kingship, as by right a man ought to behave towards his lord and master. May God and the saints, whose relics lie here before me, grant me their help; for to this end I shall devote and consecrate myself with all the intelligence that God has given me, for the remainder of my life.*

Next to fighting battles, traveling was one of the most dangerous things a Carolingian could do. The following letter, written in the 800s by a clergyman named Lupus of Ferrières, describes the hazards of the road:

*To his dearest Reg. Lupus sends greetings in the Lord.*

*We long for your arrival, as is fitting, for certain letters have already bespoken your coming. But we urge you to choose a route with the most vigilant [watchful] caution, because in the reign of our king Charles, when disturbances arise, robberies are committed . . . [without fear of punishment], and nothing happens more surely and more often than violent plundering. You must therefore seek such a group of fellow travelers whose number and courage will prevent the acts of the brigands [robbers] or repulse them, if necessary. . . .*

*I wish you the best of health and good luck.*

Most Carolingian peasants were very superstitious. Sometimes the charms they muttered were the same as those their ancestors had used. The Church changed many charms by substituting "God" or "Christ" for "Father Heaven," and "the Virgin Mary" for "Mother Earth." The following spell is one that beekeepers used to prevent a swarm of bees from flying away:

*Christ, there is a swarm of bees outside,*
*Fly hither, my little cattle,*
*In blest peace, in God's protection,*
*Come home safe and sound.*
*Sit down, sit down, bee,*
*Saint Mary commanded thee.*
*Thou shalt not have leave,*
*Thou shalt not fly to the wood.*
*Thou shalt not escape me,*
*Nor go away from me.*
*Sit very still,*
*Wait God's will!*

Carolingians were superstitious about many things in addition to beekeeping. Einhard, who served as Charlemagne's secretary, adviser, and personal friend for more than twenty years, described the strange happenings that seemed to foretell the king's death:

*Many portents marked the approach of Charlemagne's death, so that not only other people but he himself could know that it was near. In all three of the last years of his life there occurred repeatedly eclipses of both the sun and the moon; and a black-colored spot was to be seen on the sun for seven days at a stretch. The immensely strong portico [fancy porch] which he had constructed between his palace and the cathedral came crashing down to its very foundations one Ascension Day. The wooden bridge across the Rhine near Mainz which he had built over a period of ten years, with such immense skill and labor that it seemed likely to last for ever, caught fire by accident and was burnt out in three hours, to the point that not a single plank remained, except what was under the water. What is more, one day during the last expedition which he led into Saxony against Godefrid, the King of the Danes, just before sunrise, as he was setting out from his camp and was beginning the day's march, he suddenly saw a meteor flash down from the heavens and pass across the clear sky from right to left with a great blaze of light. As everyone was staring at this portent and wondering what it meant, the horse which Charlemagne was riding suddenly lowered its head and fell, throwing him to the ground so violently that the buckle fastening his cloak was broken and his sword-belt torn away. He was picked up, without his arms and his cloak, by*

This silver
coin portrays
Charlemagne
as an ancient
Roman.

the attendants who were near and ran to his aid. Even his
javelin, which he was holding tightly in his hand, fell from his
grasp and lay twenty feet or more away from him.

There were frequent earth-tremors in the palace at Aachen;
and in the apartments where Charlemagne lived the wooden
beams of the ceiling kept on creaking. The cathedral in which he
was subsequently buried was struck by lightning and the golden
apple which adorned the highest point of the roof was dashed off
by a thunderbolt and thrown on the top of the Bishop's house,
which was next door. In the cathedral itself . . . there was written
in red ochre an inscription which recorded the name of the man
who had constructed it. The words Karolus Princeps [Prince
Charles] were included in the first phrase. In the very year of
Charlemagne's death, only a few months before he died, people
noticed that the lettering of the word Princeps was beginning to
fade and that it eventually became illegible.

# Glossary

**anoint:** To put oil on a person during a religious ceremony.

**Carolingian:** The dynasty to which Charlemagne belonged.

**catapult:** A weapon that hurls large stones or spears.

**clan:** A group of related families.

**classical:** Referring to ancient Greece or Rome.

**consecrate:** To devote to a good purpose; to declare something sacred or holy.

**dowry:** The money or property that a bride brings to a marriage.

**embassy:** A diplomatic mission to a foreign government or ruler.

**envoy:** A person sent on a diplomatic mission by a government.

**epic:** A long poem that tells of the adventures of heroes in legend or history.

**Gregorian chant:** A chant with a single musical line that was used in public Christian worship during the Middle Ages.

**guerrilla warfare:** An irregular type of warfare consisting of raids and ambushes rather than pitched battles.

**hogshead:** A large cask or barrel.

**javelin:** A five-foot-long wooden spear with an iron point; when a javelin struck a shield, the point would bend at the neck, thus preventing the enemy from pulling the spear out and throwing it back at the attacker.

**lay; layman:** Not a part of the clergy; a person not part of the clergy.

**manuscript:** Hand-written material.

**monastery:** A community of men or women who devote themselves to prayer, study, and work; also, the buildings that house such a community.

**mosaic:** A design made by inlaying small colored pieces of stone, tile, or marble into a surface to create a picture or pattern.

**Muslim:** A follower of the religion of Islam.

**ochre:** Earthy iron compound used as a coloring agent.

**pagan:** Someone who is not a Christian, a Jew, or a Muslim.

**perjury:** Violating an oath or vow by swearing to something that is untrue.

**portent:** A sign that foretells a coming event.

**relics:** Objects of religious respect, especially bones or personal items from the body of a saint.

**scribe:** A writer.

**steward:** The manager of another's property.

**tunic:** A long, loose-fitting garment, either sleeved or sleeveless, often worn belted at the waist.

# For Further Reading

Asimov, Isaac. *The Dark Ages.* Boston: Houghton Mifflin, 1968.

Banfield, Susan. *Charlemagne.* New York: Chelsea House, 1986.

Biel, Timothy Levi. *The Importance of Charlemagne.* San Diego: Lucent Books, 1997.

Brooks, Polly Schoyer, and Nancy Zinsser Walworth. *The World of Walls.* Philadelphia: J. B. Lippincott, 1966.

Corrick, James A. *The Early Middle Ages.* San Diego: Lucent Books, 1995.

Hinds, Kathryn. Life in the Middle Ages: *The Countryside.* New York: Marshall Cavendish, 2001.

———. Life in the Middle Ages: *The Church.* New York: Marshall Cavendish, 2001.

Komroff, Manuel. *Charlemagne.* New York: Julian Messner, 1964.

Lebrun, Francoise. *The Days of Charlemagne.* Morristown, NJ: Silver Burdett, 1986.

Rowling, Marjorie. *Everyday Life in Medieval Times.* New York: G.P. Putnam's Sons, 1968.

Winston, Richard. *Charlemagne.* New York: American Heritage, 1968.

# Bibliography

Biel, Timothy Levi. *The Importance of Charlemagne.* San Diego: Lucent Books, 1997.

Bishop, Morris. *The Horizon Book of the Middle Ages.* New York: American Heritage, 1968.

Brooks, Polly Schoyer, and Nancy Zinsser Walworth. *The World of Walls.* Philadelphia: J. B. Lippincott, 1966.

Cantor, Norman F. *The Civilization of the Middle Ages.* New York: HarperCollins, 1993.

———, ed. *The Medieval Reader.* New York: HarperCollins, 1994.

Creekmore, Hubert, ed. *Lyrics of the Middle Ages.* New York: Grove Press, 1959.

Einhard and Notker the Stammerer. *Two Lives of Charlemagne,* translated by Lewis Thorpe. New York: Penguin Putnam, 1969.

Gies, Frances, and Joseph Gies. *Cathedral, Forge, and Waterwheel: Technology and Invention in the Middle Ages.* New York: Harper-Collins, 1994.

Grant, Michael. *Dawn of the Middle Ages.* New York: McGraw-Hill, 1981.

Heer, Friedrich. *Charlemagne and His World.* New York: Macmillan, 1975.

Komroff, Manuel. *Charlemagne.* New York: Julian Messner, 1964.

McKay, John P., et al. *A History of Western Society,* 2nd ed. Boston: Houghton Mifflin, 1983.

Power, Eileen. *Medieval People.* New York: Barnes & Noble, 1963.

Riché, Pierre. *Daily Life in the World of Charlemagne,* translated by Jo Ann McNamara. Philadelphia: The University of Pennsylvania Press, 1978.

Rowling, Marjorie. *Everyday Life in Medieval Times.* New York: G. P. Putnam's Sons, 1968.

Singman, Jeffrey L. *Daily Life in Medieval Europe.* Westport, CT: Greenwood Press, 1999.

Wedeck, Harry E., ed. *Putnam's Dark and Middle Ages Reader.* New York: G. P. Putnam's Sons, 1964.

Winston, Richard. *Charlemagne.* New York: American Heritage, 1968.

# Notes

### Part One: A Mighty Monarch

Page 10. "May the king": Komroff, *Charlemagne*, p. 22.
Page 11. "the faithless and stinking Lombards": Komroff, *Charlemagne*, p. 29.
Page 17. "who had conquered many lands": Brooks and Walworth, *The World of Walls*, p. 57.
Page 32. "To Charles, Augustus": Heer, *Charlemagne and His World*, p. 139.
Page 35. "to develop along common paths": Biel, *The Importance of Charlemagne*, p. 113.

### Part Two: Everyday Life in the Time of Charlemagne

Page 39. "not with a voice": Riché, *Daily Life in the World of Charlemagne*, pp. 235–236.
Page 42. "a pious action": Riché, *Daily Life in the World of Charlemagne*, p. 276.
Page 44. "Let no one in the monastery": Brooks and Walworth, *The World of Walls*, p. 20.
Page 45. "the enemy of the soul": Cantor, *The Medieval Reader*, p. 39.
Page 47. "It is cold": Gies, *Cathedral, Forge, and Waterwheel*, p. 78.
Page 47. "turn the pages gently": Rowling, *Everyday Life in Medieval Times*, p. 28.
Page 52. "Shortages could be caused": Riché, *Daily Life in the World of Charlemagne*, p. 48.
Page 55. "to cast or break spells": Gies, *Cathedral, Forge, and Waterwheel*, p. 62.
Page 57. "Let us make use": Riché, *Daily Life in the World of Charlemagne*, p. 177.
Page 59. "What is the use": Einhard and Notker the Stammerer, *Two Lives of Charlemagne*, p. 133.
Page 64. "purple and silken robes": Power, *Medieval People*, p. 37.
Page 65. "carrying for the army": Power, *Medieval People*, p. 30.

### Part Three: The Carolingians in Their Own Words

Page 68. "I and Pangur Ban": Creekmore, *Lyrics of the Middle Ages*, pp. 198–199.
Page 70. "Two priests followed": Cantor, *The Medieval Reader*, pp. 52–53.
Page 71. "What is the sun?" Wedeck, *Putnam's Dark and Middle Ages Reader*, p. 264.
Page 72. "I promise that": Rowling, *Everyday Life in Medieval Times*, p. 18.
Page 73. "To his dearest Reg": Wedeck, *Putnam's Dark and Middle Ages Reader*, pp. 268–269.
Page 73. "Christ, there is a swarm of bees": Power, *Medieval People*, pp. 28–29.
Page 74. "Many portents": Einhard and Notke the Stammerer, *Two Lives of Charlemagne*, pp. 84–86.

# Index

Page numbers for illustrations are in **boldface**